TRAINING TO SUCCEED

Track Athletics

Rita Storey

FRANKLIN WATTS
LONDON • SYDNEY

First published in 2009 by
Franklin Watts
338 Euston Road
London NW1 3BH

Franklin Watts Australia
Level 17/207 Kent Street
Sydney NSW 2000

Words in **bold** are in the glossary on page 31.

Series editor: Sarah Peutrill
Art director: Jonathan Hair

Series designed and created for Franklin Watts by Storeybooks.
Designer: Rita Storey
Editor: Nicola Edwards
Photography: Tudor Photography, Banbury

Picture credits
© 2007 Getty Images p27, © 2004 Getty Images pp19 and 29; Oaklands Athletics Academy pp 7, 17 and 24.

Cover images: Tudor Photography, Banbury.

Every attempt has been made to clear copyright. Should there be any inadvertent omission please apply to the publisher for rectification.

Thanks to Gary Anderson – performance director at Oaklands Athletics Academy for all his help, and to Oaklands Athletics Academy for the use of their facilities. Also thanks to Bunmi, Chantelle, Rhys and Ronnie for their participation in the book.

A CIP catalogue record for this book is available from the British Library.

Dewey classification: 796.42
ISBN: 978 0 7496 8430 3

Printed in China

Franklin Watts is a division of Hachette
Children's Books, an Hachette UK company.
www.hachettelivre.co.uk

Contents

Meet the athletes

Track athletics is made up of a range of competitive events, from short sprints to long-distance marathons. The races usually take place on an athletics track, either outdoors or indoors. For most people their experience of track athletics will be just for fun, but for a few talented individuals athletics will also become their career. In this book you will meet four athletes who dream of turning their talent into a professional career. They will share with you their experiences of the training and dedication it takes to perform at the highest level.

Go for gold

The ultimate prize for a track athlete is a gold medal at the Olympic Games. The modern Olympic Games began in 1896 but track athletics can trace its origins back to the Olympic Games of ancient Greece, which were held more than 2,500 years ago.

Ronnie Sparke

I am seventeen years old and I am a long distance and cross country runner. I love the element of individual competition in athletics. There is only one winner and it feels great to win. I also enjoy the training and the friends that you make.

Coach's comment
Ronnie represented England at the World Schools Cross Country Championships finishing a very creditable 5th overall. He was ranked 3rd overall in the UK over 1,500m last year.*

* This is from the POWER of 10 ranking system for last year in the UK. These are age group based.

Chantelle Bazzoni

I am seventeen years old and I am an 800m runner. I love athletics because of the challenge it gives me. I get a real feeling of accomplishment after a good training session and I enjoy competing. I like competing as an individual but I still feel that athletics is a team sport and I enjoy supporting other team members.

Coach's comment
Chantelle is one of our most dedicated young athletes. Initially she failed to reach the performance targets we set, but she never gave up. That persistence has led to her having the biggest percentage improvement of all our athletes in 2007/2008 and she is now one of our leading performers.

Bunmi Awokoya

*I am seventeen years old and I am a **heptathlete**. In my sport I take part in seven different events. I have to run two different distances (200m and 800m) as well as take part in a sprint **hurdle** race. I also have to compete in javelin, shot put, high jump and long jump. I like this event, as I am good at all the different sports. I don't think that I would be so good at just one. I love athletics because I enjoy improving my times and distances.*

Coach's comment

Bunmi is a very exciting prospect who has improved considerably over the winter. She was ranked 12th in the UK last year.* She has just made her debut in the UK Senior Women's League.

* This is from the POWER of 10 ranking system for last year in the UK. These are age group based.

Rhys Glastonbury

*I am seventeen years old and I am a **middle distance** runner. I have played lots of different sports including cricket, football, rugby and swimming. I enjoy athletics because I love the competition and training and I love to win. Athletics also has a good social side, which I enjoy.*

Coach's comment

Rhys is the Welsh indoor champion over 1,500m and has represented Wales over cross-country during the past winter. He is ranked 8th in the UK over 1,500m.*

* This is from the POWER of 10 ranking system for last year in the UK. These are age group based.

All these athletes are hoping to compete at the very highest level. Some may achieve their dream, but others may not be so lucky.

5

Starting out

Young people who want to try athletics can choose from a variety of different events until they find one that suits them. Each type of race needs different abilities. Short sprint races need explosive bursts of speed, middle distance races are fast and tactical, and long distance races are a test of endurance and stamina.

School and clubs

Most athletes start taking part at school and then join an athletics club. Athletic clubs have **coaches** who help you train. They encourage you to take part in competitions and will enter you in races at the right level for your ability. A track athletic race is usually a battle between individual athletes, so having other club members to cheer you on can help your confidence.

I didn't start taking part in athletics until I started secondary school. My school entered me in a 100m race and a shot put competition and I won, so I carried on competing. My dad used to take part in athletics when he was my age in Africa and my sister takes part too.

At first I felt really nervous when I was competing because I thought I might lose, but as I got more confident and made friends I started to really enjoy competing.

Both my sisters do athletics at a high level; they have both run for Great Britain and all my family have encouraged me. I started running with my sisters just for fun, then I realised that I was good. I won a cross-country league and continued to compete after that.

Track athletics main events

Sprints
60m (indoors)
100m
200m
400m

Middle distance
800m
1,500m

Long distance
5,000m
10,000m

Marathon
42.195km

Race Walking
10km
20km
50km

Hurdles
100m (women)
110m (men)
400m

Steeplechase
3,000m

Relay
4x100m
4x400m

Multiple events
Pentathlon
Heptathlon
Decathlon

Training schemes

Schemes, such as star:track and Youth Sport Trust in the UK and Little Athletics and Athletics for the Outback in Australia, run coaching programmes to help young athletes with their training.

I didn't do athletics at junior school but I took part in just about every other sport. I started athletics with cross-country running for my senior school. I was really scared when I ran my first race, but I was so happy when I found out that I had won that I couldn't wait to compete again.

Academies

Athletes with talent and dedication to compete at a high level may be accepted at a sports academy. Academies allow students to develop their talent at the same time as pursuing their academic studies.

The four athletes featured in this book are training at the Oaklands Athletics Academy in St Albans, but they still compete as members of their athletics club as well as for the academy.

I started taking part in athletics at school and then I joined a club. My dad was a Great Britain junior international middle distance runner and he taught me to believe in myself. When I first started to compete I didn't know what to expect and I was really nervous. I joined a club and had a coach to help me and I started to improve very quickly.

International events

Top athletes run qualifying races and the best are picked to represent their country at international events such as the World Championships, the European Championships, the Pan-American Games and the Commonwealth Games.

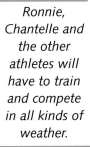

Ronnie, Chantelle and the other athletes will have to train and compete in all kinds of weather.

The coach

One of the most important people in an athlete's life is his or her coach. Coaches work closely with athletes to help them analyse and improve their technique. The coach is responsible for not only the physical development and training of the athletes, but also for giving them a positive attitude and the belief that they can succeed.

The role of the coach

A coach's job is to allow athletes to reach their maximum potential at just the right rate. To do this, coaches monitor every aspect of the athletes' performance and develop a training programme that will increase their fitness and improve their technique. Over-training could mean that an athlete gets injured, so it is important to progress at the correct pace.

Gary Anderson
(performance director at Oaklands Athletics Academy)

Gary is a UK Athletics level 4 Performance coach and studied coaching at postgraduate level. He has worked with Olympic athletes from a number of sports. His coaching philosophy is "athlete centered - coach led" with emphasis on producing a well-conditioned athlete both physically and mentally.

Gary watches Chantelle as she works on a change to her running style to help her get more power out of each stride.

Performance analysis

Coaches use a variety of different methods to get the best out of their athletes. They use video equipment to film races so that they can be played back and analysed. If a race has gone badly, slowing down the action makes it possible to identify the exact moment when things went wrong and to discuss how to improve.

Gary and Chantelle watch video footage of an 800m race and discuss tactics.

Coach's notes: responsibility

A good coach and the proper training facilities are both important, but all the support networks in the world will not make you a good athlete unless you take a level of responsibility for your own lifestyle.

My coach is from South Africa. He is a highly qualified athletics coach, a **physiotherapist** and also a qualified dance coach. He helps me to relax and have confidence in my ability. He makes me visualise a race before I run it and then we watch video footage of the race afterwards to analyse my technique.

Bunmi's coach Graham is trying to improve how straight she runs by getting her to run along one of the lines on the track instead of inside her lane.

My coaches are also my classroom teachers and I get on really well with them. They help me identify targets and aims. Before a competition we go through everything that I need to think about.

In training

As well as the specific training needed for each type of different race, athletes need to become generally very fit. Being fit reduces the risk of injury.

General fitness

Once athletes begin to train seriously to compete in an event, their coach will give them individual strength and fitness programmes to follow. Athletes use a range of exercises to strengthen their muscles and bring their bodies to a high level of general fitness and flexibility. This can mean regular training sessions in the gym as well as on the track.

When races are determined by a hundredth of a second, it is easy for us as coaches to explain why every training session is important.

Coach's notes: training

Training as a track athlete is very demanding. If you look after your body you are much less likely to get injured when you are training or competing. You need to eat a well balanced diet, drink lots of water and get plenty of rest.

*These **circuit exercises** in the gym are used to increase general levels of fitness. Coaches supervise the session.*

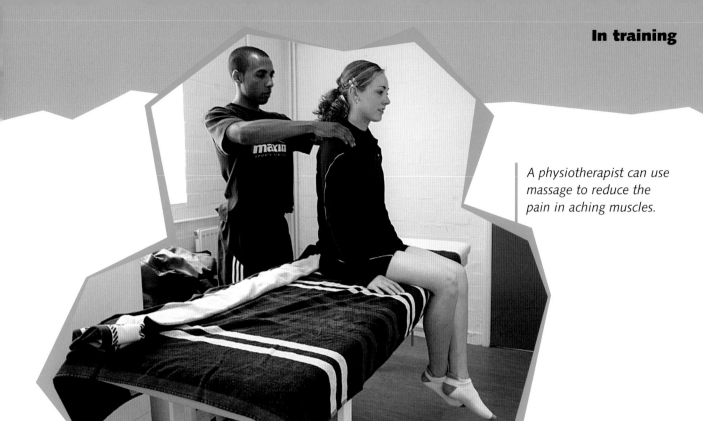

A physiotherapist can use massage to reduce the pain in aching muscles.

Warm up and cool down

Before training or competing, all track athletes do a series of stretches and drills to get their muscles ready for working at their maximum and to prevent any muscle damage. Once the race or training session is complete they do another set of stretches to 'cool down'. These stretches allow the muscles to relax and prevent them from stiffening up and causing cramp.

Aches and pains

The training programmes that athletes follow will push their bodies further and further as their performances improve. This will inevitably mean some aches and pains. The specially trained physiotherapist who looks after the athletes can sort out minor injuries, as well as helping athletes recover from more major ones.

Training the mind

It is important for athletes to have a positive approach to every race and believe that they can win. A **sports psychologist** can work with an individual to help them have the right mental attitude and self-belief to succeed.

I get very nervous before competitions. My coach has encouraged me to work with a sports psychologist to help me believe in my own abilities and have more self-confidence.

Long distance race training

To be able to compete in long distance races athletes need a great deal of stamina. They also need tactical skill. Runners have to conserve some energy in case they need to sprint to the finish at the end of an exhausting race. If a competitor is alongside you all the way, the outcome may be decided by whoever has enough energy over the last few metres.

Training sessions

Ronnie's coach has worked out a training programme for him that is different each day. Some days may involve a steady run, while others are a combination of walking, easy running and sprinting with only a short period between each to recover.

This type of training helps Ronnie to run at a consistent speed but also have the ability to change pace as necessary. A typical training session might be a 600m run followed by a 400m, 300m and 200m run with a two minute break between each. The speed and technique of each run is different and in a race Ronnie may need to combine all of them without any break in between.

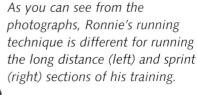

As you can see from the photographs, Ronnie's running technique is different for running the long distance (left) and sprint (right) sections of his training.

Split seconds count
In the final of the 10,000m at the 2000 Sydney Olympics Haile Gebrselassie of Ethiopia beat his rival, Kenya's Paul Tergat, by nine-hundredths of a second.

Ronnie trains less in the gym than a sprinter or middle distance runner. Most of his training is on the track or across country. The emphasis is on stamina and flexibility, rather than on building muscle.

Cross-country

Long distance runners often compete in cross-country events during the winter. These races are over a set course and distance. They are run in almost all weathers and in conditions that may be cold, wet, muddy and slippery.

Thinking while you run

Determination and self-belief are vital to running long races and being mentally as well as physically tough is essential. Before a race, a runner will have a race plan worked out based on the other competitors and their style of running. Depending on the pace of the race and who is in the lead, that plan may need to be changed more than once as the race progresses.

Long distance training takes a long time. I train at least six times a week for about an hour as well as doing a long run once a week. I normally run in the morning so that I can spend the rest of the day on college work and seeing friends. As I am improving, the amount of time I need to train for is increasing.

Ronnie's times in training and races are stored in the computer so that he and his coach can monitor his progress.

Heptathlon training

A heptathlete takes part in seven different events. The track elements of a heptathlon are the 100m hurdles and the 200m and 800m races. There are also four field athletics events: high jump, shot put, long jump and javelin.

Sprints

The 100m hurdles and 200m race are both sprints. These are two of the fastest of all athletics races and need explosive power over a short distance. Sprint athletes need very powerful leg and arm muscles. Training for sprints includes fitness training in the gym and on the track to increase muscle power in the legs and arms. Sprint athletes also need training to increase their stamina so that they can maintain the maximum speed right to the end of the race.

Sprint races are run in lanes marked on the track and the athletes start the races from **starting blocks**. Getting the best possible start to a sprint race is vital if an athlete is to have a

Decathlon

The combined event that men compete in is called the decathlon. This event involves ten track and field events. Events are held over two days and the winner is calculated by the combined results in all the events. Traditionally, the title of 'World's Greatest Athlete' has been given to the man who wins the decathlon.

Graham the coach supervises in the gym as Bunmi uses weights to increase the power in her leg and arm muscles.

This piece of equipment is called a sled. It is used to develop the leg drive. Extra weights can be added as the athlete's fitness improves.

chance of winning. Athletes spend a lot of time perfecting their starting technique from the blocks.

Once an athlete is out of the blocks, there are three phases to the race. The **acceleration** phase, where the athlete drives forward to build up speed, the stride phase, which is relaxed and smooth and then the lift phase, which uses a high knee action and fast arms towards the finish.

If a race is longer than 100m, the athletes also practise running the bends on the track without stepping outside their lane. If athletes step outside their lane during a race they are **disqualified**. They also train to perfect their running style and their finish.

Hurdles

The 100m hurdles race involves all the elements of a sprint with the added difficulty of clearing ten hurdles placed at regular intervals in their lane. A hurdler practises to create an even, flowing stride pattern so that he or she can clear the hurdles as quickly as possible without interrupting the speed of the sprint.

Bunmi practises getting as low as she can over each hurdle.

800m

This middle distance race needs not only speed but also stamina and tactics (see pages 16 and 17).

Each of my training sessions is dedicated to one event. Sometimes if I can't get an event right I have to use another session to practise, which takes up a lot of time.

Middle distance training

Middle distance races are a test of speed, strength and determination. Athletes who run this distance need to have the endurance of a long distance runner, as well as the strength and speed of a sprinter.

Endurance training

Endurance training is used to help an athlete run for long periods. In middle distance running this helps when there are a number of **heats** before the final. Endurance training is slower than race pace and takes place over longer distances.

Strength and flexibility of the quad muscles (front of the thigh), hamstrings (back of the thigh) and calves are important in middle distance running. Rhys stretches these muscles before every training session.

Speed training

The technique of sprinting is practised at slow speeds and then transferred to runs at full speed. The training at full speed will mean a series of fast sprints with a short recovery period between them.

Chantelle trains in the gym to increase the strength in her leg muscles.

I enjoy the tactical side of middle distance racing, it's very exciting. Running middle distance means there is a lot of variety in my training sessions as I need a combination of speed and stamina. I like the speed training but I don't enjoy the endurance sessions on the track quite so much.

The start

In an 800m race, athletes run twice around the track. The competitors start the race in a standing position. They must run the first 100m in their own lane, but from then on they need to find the best position on the track.

Having a race plan

Before a race, runners study their opponents' recent form and work out a race plan. They decide where they need to be positioned at each stage of the race. Towards the end of a race, a bell is rung to let the runners know that they have one lap left to go. At that point they must get into the best possible position on the track. If an athlete gets surrounded by other runners and is not able to move out to overtake them it is called being 'boxed in'.

Very few athletes lead the race and go on to win. Most prefer to run closely behind the leaders, but must be careful not to tread on their heels. With 200m left to run, good positioning on the track allows an athlete to 'kick' (increase the pace) for a sprint to the finish line.

Rhys has positioned himself just behind the leader ready to overtake later in the race.

Middle distance runners keep an upright body position and try to relax so that they use up as little energy as possible.

Middle distance events are the hardest to train for because they need speed, endurance and a lot of mental strength. There is a lot to think about but in the end you are the only person to blame if it goes wrong!

Injuries and setbacks

All athletes suffer setbacks at some time – they may pick up an injury or experience a loss of form. It may not be the setback itself that causes the lasting harm to an athlete's career, but rather how he or she deals with it.

Injuries

Getting over an injury can be a mental as well as a physical task. A specialist physiotherapist can work on the physical aspects of getting an athlete back to full fitness after injury. The coach is important too, to help motivate and reassure the athlete at a difficult time. Returning to training too quickly after an injury could result in an even worse problem which may harm the athlete's ability to perform at the highest level. That is why it is very important to be patient and get back to full fitness gradually.

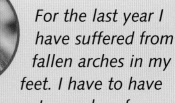

For the last year I have suffered from fallen arches in my feet. I have to have them strapped up for competitions. For a while I wasn't allowed to train because of my injury. It was horrible to have to watch everyone else training when I couldn't. I've never felt like giving up though – I always try and compete to the best of my ability, even if it is painful. I do sometimes wonder if my injury may stop me running eventually if it doesn't get sorted out.

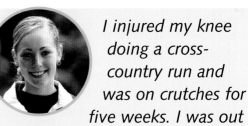

I injured my knee doing a cross-country run and was on crutches for five weeks. I was out of athletics for six months and the only training I could do was swimming. It felt as though something was missing from my life and I couldn't wait to get back to running.

A specialist sports physiotherapist examines Chantelle's injured knee.

I was injured last season. I had shin splints. I didn't run but I could train on the bike machines in the gym for an hour, four days a week. I had to put ice on my leg every day. I was lucky that it was at the start of the season and there were no major competitions so I didn't miss much.

Coach's notes: injuries

As an athlete injuries are a 'hazard of the job'. It is important that if you feel an injury coming on you seek specialist advice immediately and act on the advice given. During a period of injury, try to stay positive, it may be you are able to focus on other areas of your conditioning.

I had a serious injury that kept me out of athletics for eight months. I broke my leg and had to take my time getting back to running. The only training I could do was swimming and light circuits. It was very frustrating. Setbacks are often for a reason and they make you more determined. If things go badly you just have to train harder. There is a saying, 'Form is temporary, class is permanent'.

Wojtek Czyz had his lower leg amputated in 2001 after a football accident. He won a gold medal in the 200m at the Paralympic games in 2004.

Loss of form

Athletes are very lucky if their training programme results in an even and steady improvement. Most will suffer from a lack of form at some stage. When this happens, their coach, sports psychologist and the other athletes around them will offer practical help, motivation and support, but the vital ingredient is the athlete's own determination to succeed.

Taking up the challenge

For some athletes an injury is not the end of their career, but just the beginning. The Paralympic Games take place in the same year as the Olympic Games and are an elite sporting event for athletes with disabilities.

Lifestyle

Balancing training, school work and seeing friends can mean some big changes in lifestyle for young athletes.

School work

Sports academies allow young athletes to balance their training with their academic studies. Oaklands Academy is aimed at athletes aged between sixteen and nineteen who will study for a BTEC National Diploma in Sports, as well as coaching in their athletic discipline. The athletes train for around two hours each morning then spend three hours studying in the afternoon. In the evening they may have a conditioning session or rehabilitation with the physiotherapist.

Keeping up with school work is vital as very few students make a full-time career from athletics. At the Oaklands Athletics Academy, athletes who are falling behind with their academic work or whose grades are slipping aren't allowed to train until they are at the level they should be. However, most athletes are

As I get better at sport, athletics has become a big part of my social life, which is a good thing as we all like the same sort of things. In the past I have missed out on lots of parties and nights out.

Our athletes have a strong desire to do well. The motivation to get up each morning and go to the track or weights room in the pouring rain and freezing cold tests everyone.

In addition to their other academic studies, these students have lessons in athlete lifestyle.

A healthy diet doesn't have to be boring. Here Chantelle is eating a lunch of cous-cous salad and fresh fruit.

I eat fairly carefully and make sure I drink plenty of water – but it doesn't stop me eating chocolate and crisps!

competitive and motivated individuals and organise themselves well so that they can achieve on the track as well as in the classroom.

Diet

All athletes learn to control what they eat. Many races use up large numbers of calories, so athletes eat more before a race to make sure that their bodies have the fuel they need. The type of food they eat will be recommended by their coach and a **dietician**.

Athletes burn so many calories during training that they do not need to restrict the amount of food they eat, but they do try to eat healthy foods. These foods include chicken and fish, as well as lots of fresh fruit and vegetables, pasta and rice. Athletes also drink lots of water.

Social life

Dedicating yourself to a sport at a young age can mean missing out on leisure time and seeing friends. Most young athletes believe that winning a race, getting a medal or achieving a **personal best** time (PB) more than make up for thc sacrifices they have to make. Athletics is a friendly as well as a competitive sport and athletes make many new friends through their sport.

Coach's notes: friends

Having a good network of friends and fellow athletes around you will make you have a much more positive attitude to your training. Friendly competition is very healthy.

Preparing to compete

The preparation for a competition has to be both mental and physical. The training for a big race is designed so that athletes are at the peak of their physical and mental fitness at just the right moment.

Warming up

Before a race, athletes perform a series of dynamic stretches (stretches done on the move), that are designed to work different groups of muscles. These exercises can improve an athlete's performance and reduce any stiffness in the muscles after the race is over. The athletes also jog to increase the heart rate to a level that is ready to race. This is called a **cardiovascular** warm-up. The exercises and drills will be slightly different depending on the event in which an athlete is competing.

Before the competition starts I warm up by jogging for five minutes and doing a series of drills. I try not to talk to people too much before a race as it can make me nervous. I stay quiet and focus on the race.

Bunmi uses this drill to warm up the muscles in her thighs ready for a hurdles race.

If it is a major race I start preparing a week before. I change totally – I eat lots of pasta and drink plenty of water and sleep well.

Before the race itself, I warm up for 50 minutes. I do all types of stretches and drills.

Chantelle is doing 'hip flexes'. This exercise loosens up the hips so that she can get the most out of every stride.

Mental preparation

As well as preparing physically, the athletes prepare mentally for a race. Some athletes follow a set routine that can include laying out their kit in a certain way or eating the same foods before a race.

The warm-up is a good time to mentally prepare for the race. Athletes learn techniques for clearing their mind and focusing on the race ahead. These techniques can involve listening to music, repeating positive phrases to themselves and visualising the race itself – running it and winning it.

I have a set routine that I follow on the morning of a race. I even eat the same things.

I warm up for a race by doing a 10-minute jog, followed by dynamic stretching, a break and then a series of drills and strides. I stretch my calves a lot because they can get very sore in track races.

The morning of a big race I eat more than I usually would. Before the race I jog for 15 minutes, then stretch my leg muscles (hamstrings, quads, calves). Then I do a series of drills. I listen to up-tempo music during my warm-up. Everyone gets nervous and they don't talk to each other much until the race is over.

Coach's notes: the 4 Cs

Remember the 4 Cs when you are training.
- Concentration – keep focused
- Confidence – believe in yourself
- Control – don't be distracted
- Commitment – keep the ultimate goal in your mind

Competing

All the training and preparation that athletes do is put to the test when they run in competitions.

Self belief

The start line of a major race is no place for doubts. To win races an athlete must believe in their ability. Nerves can make athletes tense and make their heart beat faster. The athlete may break into a cold sweat and find it hard to concentrate on running the race. Knowing that they have performed well in training and that they are fit and well prepared is important for controlling nerves.

Athletes need to be totally focused on what they are doing and not allow any distractions. Being able to block out the noise of the crowd and the other competitors can be a real challenge. Focusing on nothing but the lane ahead of you is sometimes called being 'in the zone'. Being in this state means that you are living in the moment and are calm and confident.

> *Being positive in a race is the key. Being in a race with people who are as quick or quicker than you can give you a good feeling. Anyone can win.*

When she is racing, Bunmi must focus on the lane ahead and block out any distractions.

Coach's notes: believe in yourself

'If you think you can you will.'

To be a winner you need to have a winning mindset. Most people don't realise what potential they have. Believing in yourself is the first step to achieving your goals.

I love running with people who are quicker or as fast as me as it makes me perform better. Personal best times are really good, but winning a major title is a great feeling.

Personal bests

As well as trying to win races, athletes constantly aim to improve their race times. Timings can vary depending on the wind conditions and the quality of the competitors. An athlete may lose a very fast race but still be delighted with the outcome if he or she achieves a personal best time.

Cooling down

After racing or training, each athlete will do a series of static stretches. These stretches are each held for at least 10 seconds. They allow the muscles to relax and the heart rate to return to normal. These stretches also reduce the amount of **adrenaline** and **lactic acid** that build up in the bloodstream when someone exercises very hard.

If I'm competing against very strong athletes it can sometimes make me very nervous and then I don't do very well. At other times it brings out the best in me. That's why it's important to have a really positive attitude before you compete. A personal best is more important to me than a medal.

The feeling I don't like is after a sprint race when I'm lying on the track trying to get the oxygen back into my system.

I use a sports psychologist to help me learn techniques to combat my nerves and help me keep focused. I like to have competition in a race to make me perform better.

Winning is not everything to me though. I believe that a new personal best is better than winning.

Ronnie takes time to stretch his muscles after a race.

Sporting heroes

Successful athletes are an inspiration to those who are working hard to reach the top of their sport. Track athletics heroes may be record-breaking world champions or Olympic medallists. Equally, they may be athletes in the same athletics club who show dedication and commitment to their event.

Success brings responsibilities

Top athletes are the focus of a lot of media attention and become role models for young people. It is important that all athletes set a positive example. Athletes damage the reputation of the sport if they cheat by taking drugs to enhance their performance. All drugs that could give an athlete an unfair advantage are banned.

Hicham El Guerrouj
(Morocco)

Olympic medals: gold: 1,500m, 5,000m (2004); silver, 1,500m (2000)

Nicknamed 'King of the mile', Hicham El Guerrouj won a gold medal in the 1,500 metres and 5,000 metres at the Olympic Games in Athens in 2004. In his athletics career before the Athens Olympics, El Guerrouj had won 84 of his 89 races.

My first athletics hero was the Moroccan Hicham El Guerrouj. Once the Australian 1,500m international runner Lacham Chisholm stayed after his training session to watch me train and talk to me about my athletics.

Dame Kelly Holmes
(Great Britain)

Olympic medals: gold: 800m, 1,500m (2004).

Dame Kelly Holmes was 34 before she finally won her Olympic gold medals after a number of injuries had robbed her of victory in other major championships. She says: 'I achieved my goals after 20 years of dreaming.'

Kelly Holmes has to be my sporting hero. She had a lot of injuries in her career but she overcame them and won a double Olympic gold. I've had a lot of injuries and I admire her determination to win and get through hard times.

Athletes are regularly tested to see if there are any illegal drugs in their bodies. An athlete who is found to have taken drugs risks being banned from the sport.

Haile Gebrselassie
(Ethiopia)
Olympic medals: gold: 10,000m, (1996, 2000)

In 2008 Haile Gebrselassie broke his own world record for the marathon, running it in a time of 2 hours, 3 minutes and 59 seconds.
He has held world records in various middle to long distance events including 2k, 5k, 10k, half marathon and 1hr runs.

My first athletics hero was Haile Gebrselassie. When I was young he was winning all the races I watched on TV. I also admire Craig Mottram because he is running with the African runners and showing that he can compete with the best of them.

Craig Mottram of Australia competes in the men's 5,000m final of the 2007 IAAF World Athletics Championships in Osaka, Japan.

The next step

Training to be an athlete is a long, slow process. Many athletes will give up before they reach the top level. Some will get injured and for others the pressures will be too much. Many will remain involved in sport in some other way, perhaps through training or coaching.

Step by step

Young athletes often begin to compete in athletics against other schools, first locally and then nationally. If they join a club, they may go on to represent their club at local, national and even international level. They will also be training to improve their personal best times and some may eventually break world records.

Bunmi, Rhys, Chantelle and Ronnie, along with the other students at the Oaklands Athletics Academy, are aiming to move on to further education that will allow them to continue their training. They are still young and have a few years to go before they begin to compete at the top level. Athletes often do not reach their peak until their late twenties or early thirties.

My ambition is to be in the Olympics one day, but before that I am aiming to go on to international competitions. I need to keep training hard and competing to the best of my ability. Perhaps one day I will be coaching other athletes.

My ambition is to go to a major championship like the Worlds or the Olympics and win a medal. In five years' time I would like to be preparing for the Commonwealth Games in 2014. Whatever happens I want to have a career in athletics.

My ambition is to represent my country and compete at the next Olympics. To get there I will need to train hard and keep improving my PBs. In four years' time I would be very proud to be wearing a Great Britain vest.

The final step

The ultimate prize for athletes all over the world is to win a medal at the Olympic Games which are held every four years. The four athletes here are aiming towards that goal, but they have a long way to go. Let's hope they make it.

My ambition is to have athletics as my job – running for Great Britain and running in major championships. To do this I am going to have to keep training very hard and competing in quick races. I would like to think that in the next five years I could be number one in Europe.

Athlete Kelly Holmes shows her two Olympic gold medals after the Athens Olympic Games in 2004.

29

Glossary

acceleration An increase in speed.

adrenaline A hormone that is released into the bloodstream in response to physical or mental stress. It stimulates the body to perform at its maximum level.

cardiovascular Involving the heart and blood vessels.

circuit exercises A workout technique involving a series of exercises performed in rotation using different pieces of apparatus.

coaches People who train athletes or athletic teams.

cross country A long race run over open country.

dietician A person who is trained to advise on healthy eating and special diets.

disqualified When a competitor is forbidden from competing because they violated the rules.

heats Contests held to decide who competes in the final.

heptathlete A person who takes part in the heptathlon; an athletic competition consisting of seven events.

hurdle A race in which contestants must leap over a number of barriers placed at intervals around the track.

lactic acid A substance produced in the muscles during exercise. Too much lactic acid can cause cramping pains.

marathon A foot race over a course measuring 42km,195m.

middle distance A track race with a distance ranging from 400m to 1,500m.

personal best (PB) A best time ever in an event.

physiotherapist A therapist who treats injuries with exercises.

sports psychologist An expert in how the mind of an athlete works. Sports psychologists help athletes believe they can win.

sprints Running races performed at high speed over a short distance.

stamina The ability to endure exhaustion.

starting blocks Angled blocks that sprinters use to help them get the fastest possible start in a race.

Find out more

Websites

www.completetrackandfield.com
Information on training for sprints, distance and hurdles events, including articles on nutrition, training and recovery and rehab.

www.olympics.org.uk/beijing2008
The official Team GB website with profiles of all the team's athletes.

www.powerof10.info
Check out the latest 10th and 100th targets for your event and age group and view previous rankings.

www.ukathletics.net/grassroots
Information on Norwich Union **star:track** – a year-round athletics experience for all children between the age of 8 and 15 regardless of ability, gender or background; **shine:awards** – opportunities for children from the age of three and upwards to try athletics through fun physical challenges and **sports:hall** – an exciting and fun athletics team game for 9–11 year olds with the emphasis on taking part and enjoyment. This site also has a club search facility to find out what's happening in your area.

www.ukathletics.net/welcome
UK Athletics works closely together with over 1,400 clubs and thousands of schools and local authorities across the UK to grow talent and ensure that athletics remains the nation's favourite Olympic and Paralympic sport.

http://news.bbc.co.uk/sport1/hi/ athletics/skills/default.stm
The BBC athletics site has a range of video masterclasses including one from heptathlete Carolina Kluft and sprint masterclasses from Asafa Powell and Colin Jackson.

www.athletics.com.au
Keep up to date with athletics in Australia including information on the Australian Sports Commission's electronic talent identification program.

Books

Know Your Sport: Track Athletics – Clive Gifford (Franklin Watts, 2006)
A guide to track events, with step-by-step photographs and explanations of some of the techniques, as well as profiles and stats giving information about some of the world's greatest athletes.

Note to parents and teachers: Every effort has been made by the Publishers to ensure that these websites are suitable for children, that they are of the highest educational value, and that they contain no inappropriate or offensive material. However, because of the nature of the Internet, it is impossible to guarantee that the contents of these sites will not be altered. We strongly advise that Internet access is supervised by a responsible adult.

Index